God's Light Shines Forth

Mike E. Robart

authorHOUSE®

1663 LIBERTY DRIVE, SUITE 200
BLOOMINGTON, INDIANA 47403
(800) 839-8640
WWW.AUTHORHOUSE.COM

© 2005 Mike E. Robart. All Rights Reserved.

No part of this book may be reproduced, stored in a retrieval system, or transmitted by any means without the written permission of the author.

First published by AuthorHouse 12/16/05

ISBN: 1-4208-9382-3 (sc)

Printed in the United States of America
Bloomington, Indiana

This book is printed on acid-free paper.

FORWARD

GODS LIGHT SHINES FORTH FOR US, This is a book of Christian poetry that I have written with the help of the Holy Spirit, I give Him all the praise and Glory. God is the most important part of my life and He should be in yours also, He leads and guides us in everything we do, without Him this world would make no sense. I can't even imagine a world without Him, if this was all there is, you live your life and then you die, nothing to look forward too, no hope in a future. What a sad feeling it is to even think about it, how do those who don't know God ever make it, what do they have to look forward too. No wonder there is so much hate and violence in the world today, it's like we live in a world where getting ahead is everything, no matter who gets hurt, or who has to pay the price. In this book I try to tell you of a loving God who cares for each one of us, we are all created equal, we all start out the same, it is the choices that we make along the way that makes each one of us different. Even though we have made bad choices we have a God who is also forgiving, He will forgive you no matter what you have done. People on death row have even asked for forgiveness and it would be granted, just like the thief on the cross. He asked Jesus to remember him when Jesus got to heaven and Jesus told him that he would be in heaven with Him. What a merciful God we serve, if you don't know Him personally then it is time you try to find Him, He will give you peace and hope, His love will come upon you and you will see what a difference He can make in your life. I hope these poems touch your heart in some way and they make you want to know God more!!

I would like to dedicate this book to the families below who have lost loved ones:

James Cresswell family-   UP IN HEAVEN
Veldon Brand   family-   DEATH
Bill Nickelson family-   SPECIAL ANGEL
Arthur Boyer   family-   R. K.
David Albert   family-   WITHOUT EXPLANATION

Also Neva Walton who has been a Sunday School teacher for over fifty years.

Titles

GODS LIGHT SHINES FORTH FOR US	2
GUIDING LIGHT	3
WE MUST SERVE GOD FOR WHO HE IS, NOT WHAT HE DOES	4
THERE IS NOTHING YOU CAN DO TODAY TO GET GOD TO LOVE YOU MORE	5
WITHOUT GOD WE CANNOT-WITHOUT US GOD WILLNOT	6
PSALM 23, 1-6	7
UP IN HEAVEN	8
ONE TERRIBLE DAY	9
DEATH	11
A SPECIAL ANGEL	12
R.K.	13
ABANDONED	15
DON'T SHUT ME OUT	16
FORGIVING SOMEONE DOES'T MAKE THEM RIGHT	17
I DID IT ALL FOR YOU	18
LIFE IS WHAT HAPPENS WHEN YOU HAVE SOMETHING ELSE PLANNED	19
REVIVALS	21
PASTOR APPRECIATION	22
A THANKSGIVING PRAYER	23
F.R.A.N.S. SUNDAY [Friends, Relatives, Acquaintances, Neighbors]	24
FIFTY YEARS-A TRIBUTE TO NEVA	25
WHAT IS THE ISAAC IN YOUR LIFE	27
JOHN THE BAPTIZER	28
NOAH	29
WHEN PROBLEMS COME	30
CHRISTIAN BROTHERS	31
WILL I HAVE A SHACK OR A MANSION WHEN I GET TO HEAVEN	33
LEARNING TO WALK	34
YOU ARE NOT BEYOND HELP	35

A RAINY DAY	36
MISUNDERSTOOD	37
LOVE	39
ONE NATION UNDER GOD	40
MOTHERS DAY	41
A FATHERS LOVE	42
A GIFT FOR ALL ETERNITY	43
BORN A BABY	45
THE ONLY WAY OUT IS THROUGH	46
HUMAN NATURE	47
ARE YOU A CRACKED POT	48
MOTIVES	49
DON'T DIE WITH YOUR MUSIC STILL IN YOU	51
I EXIST FOR YOU	52
WHY DO WE SIN	53
I JUST KEEP HAMMERING AWAY	54
WHEN YOU CAN'T SEE GOD TRUST HIM ANYWAY	55
THE CROSS	57
MY JOY IS NOT SOMEONE ELSES RESPONSIBILITY	58
NOT MY WILL BUT YOURS BE DONE	59
HE CAN WORK IT OUT	60
A LOVE LETTER FROM JESUS	61
THERAPY FOR THE HEART	63
A PRAYER FOR HEALING	64
MIRACLES STILL HAPPEN	65
BE HAPPY WITH YOURSELF	66
A PRAYER OF BEAUTY	67
THE NEW CORVETTE	69
FEATHERS IN THE WIND	70
THE HUNDRED DOLLAR BILL PRINCIPLE	71
THREE SHATTERED DREAMS	72
GOOD LUCK OR BAD	73
IN TIMES LIKE THESE	75
SAFELY HOME	76
GONE BUT NOT FORGOTTEN	77
WITHOUT EXPANATION	78
IF ONLY YOU COULD SEE HEAVEN	79

IN HIS PRESENCE	81
YOU ARE NO SURPRISE TO GOD	82
YOU DO YOUR BEST- I'LL DO THE REST	83
YOUR WILL	84
SEEKING	85
IN THE BEGINNING	87
RIGHT OR WRONG	88
HOLY-HOLY-HOLY	89
GOD BELIEVES IN YOU-HE CANT BE WRONG	90
THE END	91

PSALM 18, 29

You indeed O Lord, give light to my lamp;
O my God, You brighten the darkness about me.

PSALM 25, 4-6

Your ways oh Lord make known to me;
teach me Your paths,
Guide me in Your truth and teach me,
for You are God, my Savior,
and for You I wait all day.
Remember that Your compassion oh Lord,
and Your kindness are from old.

PSALM 27, 1-2

The Lord is my light and my salvation,
whom shall I fear?
The Lord is my refuge, whom shall I be afraid?

PSALM 119, 105

Your word is a lamp to my feet,
A light to my path.

PSALM 121, 1-2

I lift my eyes toward the mountains;
where shall my help come from?
My help is from the Lord, who made
Heaven and Earth.

Mike E. Robart

GODS LIGHT SHINES FORTH FOR US

When our lives seem dark and empty, God lights our way,
When our hearts are heavy burdened, God gets us through each day.
When we have fallen and can't get back up, He reaches down His hand,
When we can't go on and turn to Him, He'll lead us as He planned.
God has a plan for our lives, but we must learn to trust,
Our spirit is often willing, but our bodies are filled with lust.
We seek the worldly treasures, we try to do things on our own,
We forget about the God who made us, and the mercy He has shown.
Our lives get so entangled, we don't know which way to turn,
And when it seems all hope is gone, we remember Gods concern.
Why can't we just keep God first, how many times must we fail,
How many times must we stumble, till we let His hand prevail?
Why do we walk in darkness, His light is there for us to see,
Why do we turn our backs on God, not facing reality!
God created us, God is love, He only wants our best,
He loves us all the same, no one is different from the rest.
But we must submit to His will, we must follow His light,
And He will surely lead us home, we are precious in His sight!
So the next time you're feeling troubled, and your world is dark and gray,
Remember Gods light shines forth for us, He will light your way!!

GUIDING LIGHT

Have you ever noticed how hard it is, to do something on your own,
It seems like every way you turn, you run into a wall of stone.
Doors get shut that once were open, opportunities fade away,
Things that you've had planned for months, now just go astray.
You try to make a special deal, but somehow it falls through,
Do you ever stop and wonder, is this something Gods wanting me to do?
I am learning more each day, that I must trust my Lord,
When I include Him in my plans, my decisions aren't that hard!
When He is behind you all the way, doors just seem to open,
Words that I've found hard to say, now are easy spoken.
If you'll just let God have control, He knows where you should go,
And if you follow Him completely, your way He will show.
So when problems start raining down on you, and things aren't going right,
Just turn to God and ask for help, He'll be your GUIDING LIGHT !!

Mike E. Robart

WE MUST SERVE GOD FOR WHO HE IS, NOT WHAT HE DOES

We must follow God at all times, even in the wilderness,
We must realize it's God, who gives us our happiness.
We can't just follow Him, when all is going right,
We must trust Him always, even when things get tight.
When every thing is going our way, it's easy to follow our Lord,
But we must learn to serve Him, especially when life gets hard!
Or how else will we act, when God gives us all we need,
Will we turn our backs on Him, and live our lives in greed.
We can't just serve our God, only when we get our way,
No we must learn to serve Him, each and every day.
God is truly love, and we must love Him in return,
We must love each other, show others our concern.
Then we will serve our heavenly Father, who created us in love,
And we will share in all His glory, in heaven up above!!

THERE IS NOTHING YOU CAN DO TODAY TO GET GOD TO LOVE YOU MORE

Have you ever set down and thought, about Gods love for you,
He loves you unconditionally, in spite of the things we do.
We show the love we have for Him, by our songs and hymns of praise,
That won't make Him love us more, though our spirits it will raise.
His ways are so much higher, we cannot comprehend,
His love is so much greater, He'll love us to the end.
I can't see how He can love a murderer, as much as you and me,
But Jesus died for everyone, and His glory they will see.
If they only repent of their wrongs, and accept Jesus as their Lord,
They too will see His glory, I sometimes find that hard.
Vengeance is Mine, says our God, I cannot be a judge,
I must forgive everyone, I cannot hold a grudge.
What if I was that murderer, I put myself in his place,
Wouldn't I want forgiveness, so I could look upon His face?
God has no favorites, each person is His child,
We can't earn His love, even if we're undefiled.
God loves us all the same, He does not pick or choose,
But it is up to each of us, if heaven we do loose,
Don't take that chance, you're Gods child, He loves us all the same,
And may you never, ever forget, the reason Jesus came.
So always try to do your best, show God that you care,
Because He first loved us, and His love He wants to share !!

Mike E. Robart

WITHOUT GOD WE CANNOT- WITHOUT US GOD WILLNOT

Without God in our lives we are helpless,
Without Jesus in our lives we are hopeless.
When things are darkest in our lives, God lights the way,
When things seem impossible to us, God keeps us from going astray.
When we have fallen or don't know which way to turn, He leads us,
When we have sinned He doesn't forsake, for He is just.
God shows us mercy, though we don't deserve it,
He gives salvation, but we must want it.
For even though He is Almighty and all Powerful, He is still God,
He gives us wills to choose, though sometimes I find that quite odd.
He could have made us to love Him, but this is not His way,
We must choose to follow Him, each and every day !
He will not say, "Do My Will", but lets us decide,
We can choose right or wrong, how do you feel inside?
God would like for everyone, to always do what's right,
For the battle between good and evil, is a constant fight.
But God will not do it all, the decision is ours to make,
He won't force His will on us, so do not hesitate.
Give your will to our heavenly Father, be all you can be,
Then you'll share in His joy and love, for all eternity !!

God's Light Shines Forth

PSALM 23, 1-6

The Lord is my shepherd; I shall not want,
In green pastures He gives me repose,
Beside restful waters He leads me; He refreshes my soul.
He guides me in right paths for His name's sake,
Even though I walk in the valley of darkness,
I will fear no evil; for You are at my side,
With Your rod and Your staff that gives me courage.
You spread the table before me in the sight of my foes,
You anoint my head with oil, my cup overflows.
Only goodness and kindness shall follow me
all the days of my life;
And I shall dwell in the house of the Lord, for
years to come!

Mike E. Robart

UP IN HEAVEN

You see my body in the casket, but that's not really me,
I am up in heaven, with all my family.
We look down, we see the pain, that you're going through,
I wish now I could help you out, like you used to do.
When I was small you helped me grow, taught me things that I must learn,
It seemed you all were always there, showed me which way to turn.
And now you must lean on each other, for I'm no longer there,
And the love I had for each of you, now you too must share.
But I am in a better place, some of you will see me again,
All of you could be with me, if you were only sorry for your sin!
I accepted Jesus when I was young, but He has been with me all along,
When I was in trouble or felt depressed, it was Him who made me strong.
It's not easy living on Earth, there are so many choices you must make,
Up in heaven God is love, and He will not forsake.
I will remain in the hearts of those, who knew me in the past,
But I can't wait, till you get to heaven, forever will it last!!

ONE TERRIBLE DAY

It started as a celebration, a meal for them prepared,
It ended that next day, when Jesus showed how much He cared.
They sat with Jesus, broke bread with Him, then they drank the wine,
They did not know how Jesus would suffer, for their sins and mine.
It started in the garden, Jesus could see what was to come,
He was tempted by the devil, to just get up and run.
How could one man bear the pain, for the sins of all,
Jesus knew that was why He came, and He must answer the call.
They came for Him with swords and spears, like He was a common thief,
Yet just weeks before they cheered, and shared in His belief.
Now they put him on trial, told false accusations and lies,
They didn't want to just punish Him, they wanted Him to DIE!
They brought Him before Pilate, he could satisfy their plan,
But Pilate found no wrong in Him, this Jesus, the son of man.
So Pilate had Him beaten, His flesh was torn away,
They placed on His head a crown of thorns, they mocked Him all that day.
But the people were not satisfied, they screamed, "Crucify Him" instead,
They didn't want Jesus to suffer, they really wanted Him dead!
So Pilate agreed to crucify Jesus, but he washed his hands clean,
The crowd screamed, "Let His blood be on us, and on all of the unseen"!
So they placed a cross upon His back, they beat and mocked Him up the hill,
Jesus fell, but He would get up, how He suffered haunts me still.
When they reached the top they laid the cross, down upon the earth,
Jesus knew this day would come, He saw it from His birth.
They placed nails in His hands and feet, they drove them in the wood,
Satan could not see how one man could suffer, but now He understood!

Mike E. Robart

Jesus triumphed over all the evil, that ever was to come,
The devil was defeated, by the death of just this ONE!
As Jesus gave up His Spirit, He paid the price for all,
And we can live forever with Him, if only we answer His call!
If you're not saved, ask Jesus for help, He will lead the way,
And He will not have suffered in vain, on that TERRIBLE DAY!!

God's Light Shines Forth

DEATH

Oh death, where is thy sting?
You may destroy this human body, but now my spirit, now it sings.
To be absent from the body ,is to be present with the Lord,
I grieve for those who are left behind, life can be so hard.
You say you hope in the resurrection, I have been assured,
Jesus prepares a place for those, who believe and keep His word.
We as humans fear you, the devil sees to that,
But my spirit rejoices with God above, heaven is where I'm at!
Death, you have no hold on us, Jesus arose and we will too,
You are not the final act, death I have no fear of you.
I know my loved ones are hurting, they hated to see me go,
But we will be together again, because God said this is so.
Death you have no hold on us, you cannot keep us down,
For Jesus lives and so do I, He shares with me His crown.
Jesus says I am the resurrection and life, and those who believe in Me,
Shall never die but live forever, for all eternity.
So death, where is thy sting, you are just a part of Gods plan,
We were meant to loose this life, but now I live again!!

Mike E. Robart

A SPECIAL ANGEL

The definition of an Angel, is someone who is good or innocent,
You had a Special Angel, I'm sure who was heaven sent.
An angel touches peoples lives, they affect us in many ways,
They may not be around for long, but we'll remember them all our days!
You may say if there is a God in heaven, why would He allow such tragedy,
He uses Special Angels like yours, to open our eyes and see,
God can see the future, He knows the life we will lead,
He provided this Special Angel, to fill a certain need.
Now He has taken her home, to be with her family and friends,
We were created for this purpose, now she lives again!
To those who are not Christians, death is such a fatal blow,
But to us who live in Jesus, death is nothing, this I know!
She lives again and you can too, if you'll accept Christ into your life,
He will give you His peace, He will take away your strife.
You may not understand why, you may question, why me Lord?
Why is life so unbearable, why is life so hard?
We don't have all the answers, we'll never comprehend,
But we must learn to lean on Him, and trust Him to the end.
Right now your heart is broken, you're in such pain and grief,
But remember your "Special Angel" lives again, she gives you hope and relief!!

R.K.

If you know R.K., you know he has a problem,
If you don't care for R.K., then you don't really know him.
His life is being re-arranged, our Father is using him today,
He tells of peace and joy, God is using him in a special way.
He has faults like us all, no one is perfect in everything,
We all have sinned and fell short, but Jesus lifts us up again.
R.K. is an example to all of us, God can use you were you're at,
R.K. may not change the world, but God can see to that!
He has touched the lives of those he has met, his family and his friends,
No one knows what God has planned, or when their lives will end.
So let us lift our voices up, let God hear our cry,
His will be done for R.K., and not to question why?
Let us give our lives to Jesus, use me as You see fit,
Let our love grow like a flame, that long ago You lit.
And let our hearts know the peace and joy, You give us every day,
As we come to lift our voices to You, for our brother in Christ, R.K. !!

Mike E. Robart

Luke 6, 37-38

Do not judge and you will not be judged,
Do not condemn, and you will not be condemned.
Pardon and you shall be pardoned.
Give and it shall be given back to you,
Good measure pressed down, running over.
For the measure you give, it shall be returned to you.

JOHN 11, 26

I am the resurrection and the life, whoever believes
in Me, though he shall die, will come to life.
And whoever is alive and believes in Me,
shall never die!

JOHN 14, 1-3

In My Fathers house are many mansions,
I go now to prepare a place for you.
If I go, I will return to take you with Me.

ABANDONED

A little baby is left on the steps of a police station, abandoned!
A child is left to grow up in an orphanage, abandoned!
A wife and young children are left on their own, abandoned!
An elderly person is put into a nursing home, no one comes for them, abandoned!
Christ is nailed on a cross to die for our sins, abandoned!
Yes there are many who go through life feeling abandoned, but Christ knows how we feel,
He was abandoned by His Father, that was part of the deal.
God cannot live where there is sin, so He had to depart,
When Jesus took the sins of all, there upon His heart!
He paid the price so we don't have too, He knows what we go through,
He bore the pain and sufferings, for me, and also for you!
He died that we may live again, if we only accept His grace,
He arose and we will rise again, to look upon His Face!
So no matter where you are in life, you need not feel alone,
Jesus is there to help you out, His power, He has shown.
You no longer need to feel abandoned, like there is no one around,
Cause Jesus is there, by your side, He'll never let you down!!

Mike E. Robart

DON'T SHUT ME OUT

You have shut me out of your life, you have turned your back on me,
I can't understand how you can do this, nor my family!
You say you are a Christian, is this the way they act,
You say you love each other, is this a Christian fact?
How can you shut me out, the child I carry is part of you,
I just don't understand, all the things you Christians do.
You say we must get married, or you will have no part,
We want to have this child together, make a brand new start.
How can you judge me, saying it is all my fault, your son was part to blame,
Why can't you just be happy for us, why can't you love it just the same?
I don't believe like you, what we have done is not wrong,
Won't you at least accept it, and help it to belong?
We have our lives to live, you can't force your will on us,
Maybe later we'll come around, and our future we'll discuss.
But please don't shut me out, this is a happy time to share,
Won't you please accept the fact, and show me that you care!
Won't you keep an open mind, not judging me wrong or right?
Can't you feel the love I have, and share in my delight,
I want you in this baby's life, a grandmother has so much to give,
I know my grandparents had a part, in the life I live.
So please don't shut me out, open your heart and see,
Soon it will be born, and we'll be a family!
I know deep down inside, you'll love it, I have no doubt,
That is why I'm asking you now, please don't shut me out!!

FORGIVING SOMEONE DOES'T MAKE THEM RIGHT

Do you have bitterness in your heart, has someone hurt you in the past
Do you have a grudge to settle, a pain that will always last?
I'm here to tell you something, I hope it sheds some light,
Forgiving someone for something, doesn't make them right!
The pain and hurt you hold inside, seldom effect their living,
Bring it to Jesus at the alter, who taught us about forgiving.
He will take the hurt away, He will take the pain,
He will show you a loving heart, He had for those when slain!
It doesn't do you any good, to hold the bitterness within,
To have an unforgiving heart, will also lead to sin.
Cast your cares upon the Lord, feel the burden lift,
Come up to the alter, do not delay, Jesus has a gift!
He wants to give a heart of love, a mind that's free and clear,
He wants to take your hurt and pain, but you must be sincere.
Let God deal with those who have hurt you, He will make things right,
He doesn't like His children hurting, we are precious in His sight!
So forgive those who have hurt you, it doesn't mean they've won,
And you will share in joy and peace, together with God's Son!!

Mike E. Robart

I DID IT ALL FOR YOU

When I get arrogant and self righteous, I look upon the cross and Jesus says,
"I did it all for you"!
When I get proud of my accomplishments thinking I can do this on my own,
I look at the crown of thorns and Jesus says, "I wear this crown for you"!
When I think I'm better than any of you, I look at the stripes upon Jesus' body,
Jesus says, "I endured these for you"!
When I say words that hurt my fellow brothers and sisters, Jesus shows me His
nailed pierced hands, they reach out to hold me, even when I turn my back on Him
When I get greedy and want it all I look at the nails in Jesus' feet, I realize, those
nails did not hold Jesus to the cross, His love did!
Jesus died for us that we may live, He paid for our salvation,
He waits for you with open arms, and a longing anticipation.
How can we look upon the cross, forgetting what He went through,
But then I feel His love in my heart, and His words saying,
"I DID IT ALL FOR YOU"!!

LIFE IS WHAT HAPPENS WHEN YOU HAVE SOMETHING ELSE PLANNED

Have you ever had a day planned, then something else comes up, THAT'S LIFE.
Have you ever been in a hurry, then get caught in a traffic jam, THAT'S LIFE.
Have you ever been in a grocery store, the cash register breaks down, THAT'S LIFE.
Have you ever been watching a special program and the electricity goes out, THAT'S LIFE.
Have you ever been in bed asleep and the phone rings, sorry wrong number, THAT'S LIFE.
Life is what happens when you have something else planned,
Sometimes it can be easy, other times more than you can stand!
We go along, we all have trials, nothing is ever the same,
We are always looking for excuses, someone else to blame.
We get up, we plan our day, these things must get done,
Do we get so busy running, that we forget about Gods Son?
After all, He's an important part, of the life we live,
Life would be so unbearable, without the peace He gives!
So plan your day, be willing to change, there is going to be some strife,
It may not happen the way you've planned, but after all, THAT'S LIFE!!

Mike E. Robart

1 PETER 3, 10-12

He who cares for life and wants to see prosperous days must keep his tongue from evil and his lips from uttering deceit. He must turn from evil and do good, seek peace and follow after it, because the Lord has eyes for the just and ears for their cry; but against evildoers the Lord sets His face!

1 PETER 5, 6-8

Bow humbly under Gods mighty hand, so that in due time He may lift you high. Cast all your cares upon Him, because He cares for you. Stay sober and alert. Your opponent the devil is prowling like a roaring lion looking for someone to devour!

REVIVALS

Now the revival is nearly over, has something touched your heart,
Are you willing to give your all, make a brand new start?
Or will every thing remain the same, Jesus could not get through,
He stands there knocking, please let Me in, I have so much for you.
I bring you peace, My love I give, but only you can let Me in,
All I'm asking in return, is to be sorry for your sin.
Most of you are My children, but there is still a few,
Who think they can make it on their own, let Me show you what to do.
I died for everyone who will ever be born, but not all will hear My voice,
I can't force My love on you, you have to make the choice.
But if you will look, upon My hands and feet, these scars I proudly wear,
They remind Me of My love for you, don't you even care?
I'll be right here by your side, as long as you still breathe,
Hoping you will open up, My grace you will receive.
Don't put it off, the decision is yours, don't wait till it's too late,
Accept Jesus tonight, do not hesitate!!

Mike E. Robart

PASTOR APPRECIATION

Pastor Mike came to us, early one summer day,
We weren't quite sure what kind of man, God sent to lead the way.
But we could tell right away, that Mike was a man of action,
It didn't take us long to see, he was the center of attraction.
He visited homes talking to people, that he had never met before,
Inviting all to come back to church, there they would learn more!
He would go to the hospitals to be with all, even though it was out of his way,
Before the tests or surgery were performed, he'd bow with us and pray.
He even comes to share the sorrow, of a loved one who has passed on,
He tries to help the hurting and lost, a job that's never done!
He leads some in a bible study, he'd like to have us all,
But it is up to each of us, we must answer Jesus' call.
He can only do so much, we must learn to do our part,
He tells us God is kind and good, and we should make a brand new start.
I believe God knew what He was doing, when He sent Pastor Mike along,
I believe he'll work with us, and help us to be strong.
So thank You Father for sending us a leader, some one that we like,
And let us all work together for You, with the help of Pastor Mike!!

A THANKSGIVING PRAYER

Father we are thankful, for all the gifts You give,
Our cars, our possessions, the places where we live.
We know all good things come from You, You bless us everyday,
But do we ever stop and think, why Jesus came our way?
He was born that Christmas night, so very long ago,
He came to Earth to set us free, to teach us how to grow.
Jesus was God, yet He was man, a servant to us all,
He didn't have to die for us, but He fulfilled His call!
Jesus taught that we must serve, if we are to live like Him,
He taught us we must seek our Father, each time we have a problem.
He taught us we should love each other, treat everyone equally,
We should set examples, for all the world to see.
So Father we come to You with thanks, we adore You and lift Your Name,
Let us always remember the reason, just why Jesus came.
And thank You for our families, and friends that we hold **dear**,
And grant a special blessing, to everyone that is here.
And thank You for those who lead us, and thank You for **our nation**,
But most of all we want to thank You, for Jesus and our **Salvation**!!

Mike E. Robart

F.R.A.N.S. SUNDAY [Friends, Relatives, Acquaintances, Neighbors]

Today you are in this house of prayer, not by accident,
You were asked by a relative or friend, but the word was heaven sent.
Jesus works in mysterious ways, He wants to get your attention,
He placed something special on my heart, that I would like to mention.
Jesus says, "I am the Way, the Truth, the Light,
No one comes to the Father, unless Me they have in sight."
Jesus came that He may save, all who call on Him,
He came not to condemn the world, but to help us with our problems.
You may not be a Christian now, or you may have been one for years,
His message is the same to all, what He says you need to hear.
"I came that you may have life, I gave My life for you,
I go to prepare a place in heaven, where you can follow too !
If anyone thirsts let him come to Me, I will give him drink,
This water is everlasting life, this is heavens link.
My house has many mansions, I go to prepare a place,
I give to you My love and peace, I give to you My grace.
Come follow Me, open your heart, please let Me come inside,
Let Me free you of all sin, this is the reason I died.
Don't put it off another day, ask Me to live in your heart,
Together we can change your life, give you a brand new start.
The Father has placed you in My hands, not one I want to loose,
But I can't decide for you, it's up to you to choose"!!

FIFTY YEARS-A TRIBUTE TO NEVA

Fifty years, it seems like a long time, but then again like yesterday,
How many bible stories have you told, as you journeyed on your way?
How many lives have you touched, how many seeds did you sow,
How many souls have been saved, only God will know!
You've been faithful in serving, many have been blessed,
Little children, now they are grown, now they face life's tests.
I wonder if they ever recall, the stories that you told,
Of Jesus' love and tenderness, their future you tried to mold.
You gave to those around you, you helped where ever you could,
You led by your example, always bringing out the good.
God has blessed you with a lovely voice, you gladly sing His praise,
How you keep your joyful heart, I am still amazed!
But Neva I'm here to tell you, God is not finished yet,
He has so much in store for you, things you'll never forget.
You may be retiring from teaching, but He's not finished with you,
He wants to be by your side, in all you say and do.
So good luck in your future, may your life be full of joy,
And may Gods blessings be on you, and His happiness you'll enjoy!!

Mike E. Robart

JAMES 1, 12-13

Happy the man who holds out to the end through trials. Once he has been proved he will receive the crown of life the Lord has promised to those who love Him. No one who is tempted is free to say, "I am being tempted by God." Surely God, who is beyond the grasp of evil tempts no one!

JAMES 4, 6-8

God resists the proud, but bestows His favor on the lowly. Therefore, submit to God; resist the devil, and he will take flight. Draw Close to God, and He will draw close to you.

WHAT IS THE ISAAC IN YOUR LIFE

Do you remember when God asked Abraham, to sacrifice his son,
Do you recall what Abraham did, and exactly what God done?
Isaac was coming between God and Abraham, so God gave him a test,
Would Abraham give his precious son, the one that he loved best!
We all have things in our lives, we don't want to give away,
Do you have something that's more important, God's asking you today.
Are you willing to give it up, to make that sacrifice,
God has to be number One, nothing else will suffice!
God gives us tests that we must pass, He must know our heart,
If He's not first in our lives, then it's time we make a new start.
We are only stewards, we don't own the homes, the cars,
God lets us use these worldly possessions, but they're not really ours!
But if we are willing to give them up, to make Him number One,
He'll do for us what He did for Abraham, when He asked him to give his son.
We must be willing to give our all, we can't hold anything back,
And He will give His all to us, there is nothing we will lack!
So make God number One, put nothing in His place,
You'll be glad you did, when you look upon His Face!!

Mike E. Robart

JOHN THE BAPTIZER

I am John the Baptist, I baptize only with water,
There is One who follows me, He is greater than any other.
I am just a voice in the desert, preparing the way of the Lord,
Jesus is the One that you must follow, to receive your heavenly reward.
I come to you saying, "Reform your lives, the reign of God is at hand,
There is One who follows me, He will make a stand."
You come to me confessing your sins, but I cannot forgive,
But the One who follows me, will show you how to live!
I called you "Brood of vipers", I questioned why you came,
You thought I was the Messiah, but we are not the same.
I am not even worthy, to loosen His sandals strap,
I am merely a bridge before Him, filling in the gap!
In Mathews gospel, chapter eleven, verse eleven I believe,
Jesus says there is no one greater, but I am quite relieved.
He goes on to say that the least, that is born into Gods kingdom,
Is greater than I, so don't you see, it doesn't matter where you're from.
I even questioned, "Are You the One, or should we expect another",
He sent me word He was doing things, greater than any other!
So now I am truly satisfied, that this is Gods own Son,
Cause no one else could know the things, and do what He has done.
I am content, I fulfilled my purpose, my journey now is done,
I go to be with our Father, I give you Jesus, Gods own Son!!

NOAH

God came to Noah, you must build a boat,
He gave him the dimensions, and said "I'll make it float".
Man has become so evil, I must destroy them all,
Noah did not question God, but immediately answered His call.
He built the boat and people laughed, they made fun of him,
He kept on working patiently, for he knew what was to happen to them.
When Noah's work was completed, God came back again,
Now load the animals and your family, cause you are without sin.
When everyone and everything was inside, the people thought they were insane,
But some began to change their minds, when it began to rain.
It rained for forty days and nights, till all on Earth was lost,
They remained in the boat for a hundred and fifty days, gently being tossed.
Then Noah sent out a dove, to find if there was dry land,
When it never returned he knew for sure, this is what God planned.
So God came to them and blessed them, saying " Be fertile and multiply",
I'll never do this again He said, and placed a bow up in the sky.
So Noah and his family started out a new,
But it wasn't long till evil raised it's head, and oh, how it grew.
But God had another plan, the Son of God was born,
He would take away our guilt, He would take our scorn!
So now we have a Savior, it's Jesus Christ our King,
And if you will accept Him, forever will you sing!!

Mike E. Robart

WHEN PROBLEMS COME

Father I'm going through a tough time, I'm not sure what I should do,
So I come to talk it over, I give my problem to You.
I'm not sure what I'm about to do, is wrong or if it's right,
But I have trust in You oh Lord, You help me see the light.
You make straight my crooked paths, You show me where to go,
You put thoughts into my head, tell me what I should know.
Father I'm learning to trust in You, more and more each day,
Cause every time I follow Your will, You show me the way.
You put me in situations, where I must make a choice,
But they become much easier, if I'll just listen for Your voice.
So Father I'm waiting to hear from You, make my choice quite clear,
Tell me what You want from me, not what I want to hear.
There's so many problems we face each day, how do You help us all,
How can You always be around, pick us up each time we fall!
I know I'm not the person yet, that You'd like me to become,
I know I haven't faced the problem, that I'm running from.
Give me guidance, show me the way, lead me where I must go,
Then maybe I can work it out, and in Your love I'll grow!!

CHRISTIAN BROTHERS

How do you re-act when you get mad, do you sometimes blow your cool,
Do you say things that you regret, maybe act like a fool?
It's hard to control your temper, when things don't go your way,
It can even sometimes be hard, to find the exact words to say.
I've been working with my emotions, but they're still hard to control,
I'd like to be calm in all situations, that is my ultimate goal.
I have learned now to just walk away, rather than get uptight,
I say a calming prayer to my Lord, I ask Him to make things right.
I give my problems to my heavenly Father, He knows what to do,
And He can handle all situations, better than me or you.
So next time you feel your blood pressure starting to rise, take a time out, or just turn and go,
Give your problems to our Lord, He will help I know.
Cause when you get mad you loose control, and say things that you don't really mean,
And words once spoken is hard to take back, this is what I've seen.
So the next time you are in this situation, think before you go to far,
People will see by your attitude, just what kind of Christian you are!
It may even have an effect, on how you treat others,
We are all Gods children, we all should be Christian Brothers !!

Mike E. Robart

1 CORINTHIANS 2, 9

Eye has not seen, ear has not heard, nor has it
dawned on man what God has prepared
for those who love Him.

REVELATIONS 3, 20

Here I stand knocking at the door. If anyone hears
My voice calling and opens the door, I will enter
his house and have supper with him and he with Me.
I will give the victor the right to sit with Me on My
throne, as I Myself won the victory and took My
seat beside My Father on His throne.

WILL I HAVE A SHACK OR A MANSION WHEN I GET TO HEAVEN

I was asked the other day, by a friend of mine,
Do you think when we get to heaven, everything will be fine?
I don't always do good works, or go to church each Sunday,
I'm not holy all the time, sometimes I forget to pray.
Do you think when I get to heaven, my reward will be the same,
What about those preachers, who tell why Jesus came.
I wasn't sure just how to answer, I had to stop and think,
Then God showed me in Mathew twenty, this became my link.
Gods kingdom is like the owner of a vineyard, who went out at the crack of dawn,
And upon reaching an agreement with workers, they went to get the work done.
He went out several more times, at different hours of the day,
And when he found workers just idle, he'd go to them and say.
You too go to my vineyard, I'll pay you what is fair,
So off they went to help the others, their burdens they would share.
And when the day was over, he started with the last,
He gave them equal pay, forgetting about their past.
I believe Jesus tells this story, this is how heaven will be,
We all will be treated equal, and His glory we will see.
We are saved by Gods good grace, not the works we do,
So my reward in heaven, won't be different than any of you!
We all will walk on streets of gold, our mansions will not lack,
And we won't have to worry, about living in some old shack!!

Mike E. Robart

LEARNING TO WALK

When I was a child learning to walk, I would stumble and fall down,
I don't remember how long it took, for me to get around.
But I never gave up I kept on trying, eventually I could stand on my own,
With each step I took it became easier, now look at me, how I've grown.
When we ask Jesus to come into our heart, it is like learning to walk again,
We don't always do what's right, we still fall into sin!
But the more I practice doing what's right, it becomes easier for me,
And the more I trust and follow my Lord, I'll become the person He wants me be.
It's not always easy to follow His ways, I still loose control,
But I know now it's the devil who tempts me, he is after my soul.
I have learned to get up after each fall, Gods grace shows me the way,
And even though I don't always do what's right, I know in His grace I'll stay.
So if you have doubt about something you've done, and you're not sure God will forgive,
Jesus has already paid the price, He died that we may live!!

YOU ARE NOT BEYOND HELP

Do you feel you've fallen so far, that no one can help you out,
Are you constantly living in fear, is your life full of doubt?
Are you in debt over your head, your money problem has got you down,
Are you so lonely, like no one cares, and no one wants you around?
I'm here to tell you Jesus cares, He is there to lift you out of your hole,
He wants to save each and every one of us, this is His ultimate goal.
But we must come to a point where we realize, we just can't make it on our own,
And He will give us His grace and peace, one which we've never known.
There's no hole too deep, or situation so impossible, He can't help us if we call,
But we must be willing to let Him handle it, let Him do it all.
For if we trust Jesus and give Him our life, there is nothing He can't do,
And you'll never feel beyond help anymore, cause Jesus will be there for you!!

Mike E. Robart

A RAINY DAY

I look outside the sky is gray, the rain is coming down,
It makes you feel so gloomy, especially when no ones around.
You sit there all alone, you wonder what to do,
Then God puts a thought inside your head, I'd like to talk to you!
So you open up your mind, what would You like to say,
Then His peace comes over you, and takes your troubles away.
For a moment in time, you're one with Him, nothing is the same,
You feel His presence all around, this is why Jesus came.
He makes us one with God, he takes away our cares,
He gives us love and peace, He teaches us to share.
Suddenly the rain gets harder, beating against the pane,
It brings you back to reality, but how you'd like to remain.
There in the presence of our God, such peace I've never felt,
All my cares and worries, they just seem to melt..
You wonder if this is how heaven will be, I can hardly wait,
To be in the presence of our loving Father, won't that be just great?
Then you hear a clap of thunder, it wakes you from your dream,
You look out and all the raindrops, now become a stream.
But the peace that you felt, it will not go away,
So give God thanks for the peace He gives, and for this RAINY DAY!!

MISUNDERSTOOD

Have you ever said one thing, and someone else took it the wrong way,
Have you ever spoken a phrase, but that's not what I meant to say.
Sometimes the words that we speak, people misunderstand,
They take them the wrong way, not the way we planned.
I have done this many times, I have been on both ends,
I have misunderstood, and I've mistaken some of my friends.
What they say is not the way, I heard it in my mind,
What they meant I never heard, sometimes we are blind.
The devil plants thoughts in our head, are you going to stand for that,
Then he twists those words around, and you're not sure where you're at.
Instead of confronting and working things out, it's easier to believe,
The twisted facts that you heard, the devil helps deceive.
Innocent words spoke without thinking, not meant for hurt or pain,
Misunderstood statements meaning no harm, now on our hearts remain.
Isn't it easy to cast all the blame, you're the reason we can't get along,
Confronting the issue is sometimes hard, but this will make us strong.
Think back now on problems you've had, have I tried to work them out,
Maybe it's only some misunderstanding, is this what the problems about?
Maybe you're saying, I'd like to work things out, if only I could,
I'm here to tell you without a doubt, it's easy to be misunderstood!
So confront the issue whatever it is, maybe you too may find,
It's simply only a misunderstanding, it will definitely ease your mind!!

Mike E. Robart

1 CORINTHIANS 13, 4-7, 13

Love is patient; love is kind, love is not jealous.
It does not put on airs, it is not snobbish,
Love is never rude, it is not self-seeking, it is
not prone to anger, neither does it brood over
injuries. Love does not rejoice in what is wrong
but rejoices in truth. There is no limit to love.
To it's trust, it's hope, it's power to endure.
There are in the end three things that last:
Faith, hope, and Love, and the greatest of these
is Love !

ROMANS 14, 12-13

Everyone of us will have to give an account of
himself before God. Therefore, we must no
longer pass judgment on one another, instead you
should resolve to put no stumbling block in your
brothers way!

LOVE

Love is patient, love is kind,
It seems like sometimes, love can even be blind.
Love is not jealous, love is not self-seeking,
Love is not boastful, when we are speaking.
Love is not prone to anger, love does not rejoice in wrong,
Love is trust and hope, love is what makes us strong.
Love carries no grudge, love does not remember pain,
Love is never rude, love keeps us from going insane.
Love is not snobbish, love never fails,
Love is forgiving, even the smallest details.
You ask me if I know what love is, it's a feeling in the heart,
Love is reaching out to someone, making a brand new start.
When I was a child, I talked like a child, I thought like a child, I acted like a child,
Now that I am grown I put aside these childish ways, but still I come back to them every once in awhile!
But I'm still human, my knowledge is imperfect, I still make mistakes,
But my love is everlasting, I will do whatever it takes!
There are three things that last, faith, hope and love,
Love is the greatest, and it comes from above.
If you had all the wealth in the world, what good would it be,
If you had not love, your life would be empty!
So yes, I know what love is, and I know what to do,
I want to share it always, and I give my love to you!!

Mike E. Robart

ONE NATION UNDER GOD

One nation under God, our forefathers knew who must come first,
They came from every country, some escaping the worst.
Religious persecution was the reason that many came,
They were all looking for something better, their outlook was the same.
They formed a brand new nation, they gave their lives to be free,
They wanted peace and a better world, for all their families.
They united in one cause, they asked God to lead the way,
He watched over them back then, like He does us today!
One nation under God, He helps us to be strong,
I sometimes wonder where we would be, if He had not helped us along.
Do you ever stop and ponder, on the history of our nation,
Do you ever stop and thank our God, who gives us all Salvation?
We have come so far, since those Pilgrims first stepped ashore,
With God leading our nation, we can accomplish so much more.
So as we celebrate the Fourth of July, and the birth of the U.S.A.,
Let us remember to thank our God, and take a moment to pray.
For all those who died that we may be free, freedom is truly a gift,
One nation under God, to Him our praises we lift !!

MOTHERS DAY

Mothers day is a special day, set aside for those who care,
Mothers are special people, their love they want to share.
Even God chose a mother, to bring forth Jesus His Son,
I think God blesses every woman, with a sense to get things done.
Just because you have born a child, does this make you a mother,
I believe it's a caring heart, a giving of one to another.
Not all women can have children, some have never been blessed,
Does this mean they have no love, are they different from the rest?
God has given every woman, that gift of a mothers heart,
Don't keep that feeling that you're alone, make a brand new start.
God has blessed all mothers, whether their family is large or small,
God also blesses all women, who answers a mothers call.
A mother will also sacrifice, the needs of her children come first,
She also gives them the benefit of doubt, never thinking the worst.
Where would we be without a mothers love, to help guide us along,
She lifts us up when we are down, she helps us to be strong.
So if you are blessed and you still have your mother, go to her and say,
Mother I love you and thank you so much, and have a wonderful,
"MOTHERS DAY"!!

Mike E. Robart

A FATHERS LOVE

When one of my sons comes to me with a problem, I try to solve it,
When one of my sons comes to me with a need, I try to help him out,
If one comes to me asking for advice, I try to share my experiences.
But what if they never came to me, does that mean I don't love them?
What if they never seek my help, or advice, or my knowledge,
Does that mean I don't care about their problems?
My love as a father is unconditional, I love them anyway,
They may not always do what I want, but who am I to say.
If we as humans want the best for our children, how much more does our heavenly Father want the best for His!
Gods ways are far above our ways, His love is greater than ours,
He created us in His own Image, sometimes we don't always do what He desires.
But does that make Him love us any less, I think not,
His love for us is unconditional, He doesn't love us for what we got!
Can you recall that wonderful feeling, when you've helped your children out,
I think our Father in heaven knows that feeling, of what life is all about.
But what if we never come to Him, how can He help us in our need,
We must learn to turn to Him, if we are to succeed.
Then He will bless us and have great joy, cause He has had a part,
He knows what we are thinking, the condition of our heart.
So when you have a problem or need, turn to your Father above,
He is there to help us out, to share in His infinite love !!

A GIFT FOR ALL ETERNITY

If I was to say I had ten envelopes here, each had a million dollars in them,
Would that be enough to help you out, could it solve your problems?
But I only have ten, whose will they be, who will decide,
I could say first come first served, would you want what's inside?
The ones in the front would have the advantage, but what about those who are fast
The strongest could surely take them away, but what about those who are last?
Isn't it strange the things we will do, to get ahead on Earth,
Isn't it sad our position in life, is determined by what we are worth!
Today I'm offering a gift to all, you don't have to be fast or strong,
It makes no difference if you're rich or poor, whether you're right or wrong.
It's a gift to all, it won't cost you a dime, would you like a brand new start,
It's called Salvation, it's free to all, just ask Jesus to come in to your heart!
It makes no difference how you have lived, the problems you've faced up to now,
Jesus will take and cast them aside, if only you will allow.
Won't you accept this gift today, open your eyes and see,
God will love you and make you His own, for all ETERNITY!!

Mike E. Robart

ROMANS 8, 38-39

For I am certain that neither death nor life,
neither angels nor principalities,
neither the present or the future, nor powers,
neither height nor depth, nor any other creature,
will be able to separate us from the love of God
that comes to us in Christ Jesus, our Lord!

ROMANS 10, 9-13

For if you confess with your lips that Jesus Christ
is Lord, and believe in your heart that God raised
Him from the dead, you will be saved. Faith in the
heart leads to justification, confession on the lips to
salvation. Scripture says, "No one who believes in
Him will be put to shame, everyone who calls on the
Name of the Lord will be saved!"

BORN A BABY

Kings brought to Him gifts of Myrrh, Frankincense and Gold,
Shepard's brought Him little lambs, taken from their fold.
Angels sang, "Glory to God, Peace upon the Earth'"
But not too many people knew, of our Saviors birth.
Born a baby in a manger, God came down to live with man,
He became a man Himself, so He could understand.
He had to learn to walk and play, He had to learn to share,
He had to feel the hurt and pain, or how else could He care?
Jesus could have been born in a palace, been born to rich and fame,
But He chose instead to live among us, that is why He came!
He humbled Himself to know our feelings, and all that we go through,
He had to experience growing up, just like me and you.
Yes Jesus came to live among us, experience what we call life,
He was tempted, abandoned, rejected, suffered all our strife.
Born to die like each of us, we all must prove our love,
But He is there to help us out, in heaven up above.
Born a baby and now a King, forever will He reign,
We just need to accept His grace, and in His love we will remain!!

Mike E. Robart

THE ONLY WAY OUT IS THROUGH

Are you facing difficulties and trials, I know I sure am,
It seems every time I turn around, I get in another jam.
I try to find a way around, I try to do things on my own,
But this is not the way it's done, you cannot do it all alone.
You have to learn to trust in God, He'll lead you through your problem,
He may not do it all, but He'll show you ways to solve them.
If you'll just listen for His voice, He's calling out to you,
You can't keep going around in circles, somehow you must go through!
I put things off for months and months, but they never go away,
I finally learned I had to face them, or they'd be here to stay.
I also learned to trust in God, He know what is in store,
We are limited by our actions, but He can do much more.
He opens doors that are closed to us, He straightens our crooked path,
It's not up to us to figure it out, let God do the math!
If you'll just learn to trust in Him, He will get you through,
It may not be the way you planned, but He know what is best for you!
So next time you have a problem, and it's more than you can face,
Ask the Lord to help you out, fill you with His grace.
He is just a prayer away, and He'll show you what to do,
Because sometimes the only way out, is the obvious, you must go through !!

HUMAN NATURE

As humans we are drawn to sin,
It didn't just happen, that's the way it's always been.
We are given choices, we can do right or wrong,
Why can't we always choose righteousness, why can't we always be strong.
God gives us all a will, it's up to us to choose,
Why do we turn our backs, His love we constantly abuse?
We say it's human nature, God will forgive us in the end,
But what about Christ's sorrows, He became our dearest friend!
He suffered so much agony, He suffered so much pain,
Did He do all this for nothing, did He die in vain?
We cannot turn and just walk away, we must stay and fight,
We can defeat this human nature, and Jesus will help us to do right.
He defeated Satan, now we must do the same,
He will give us the grace we need, show us how He overcame.
Jesus was also human, He was tempted like us all,
But He never gave in to human nature, He fulfilled His call.
So we as humans must make a stand, we must do our part,
We cannot give in to human nature, allow Jesus inside your heart.
He will help us win our battle, He's been through it all before,
And we will share in all His glory, in heaven forever more !!

Mike E. Robart

ARE YOU A CRACKED POT

Have you had problems in your life, you've tried to handle on your own,
Does it seem there's no solution, now the problems grown?
It seems we all have trials, things don't always go our way,
But some just seem to grow much larger, each and every day.
Finally they get so heavy, our spirits start to break,
We're not quite sure just how much more, we can actually take!
It's then we say, I've had enough, I can't take this anymore,
Do you know you can turn to God, He'll give you the strength to endure.
It seems sometimes we never learn, God has to break us before we see,
I know I have been cracked or broken, but now He's helping me!
I have learned to trust Him, He has our life planned out,
He created this world, this universe, should I have any doubt?
He will get me through this mess, like He's done before,
And I will give Him praise and glory, Him will I adore.
If you were to place a lighted candle, in a pot that is whole,
You would never see it's light, it's brightness you would never behold.
Sometimes we must be broken, to let the light of God shine through,
We can't always do it ourselves, let God show you what to do.
Then give Him the praise and glory, don't be something that you're not,
And remember always, God can use you too, even if you are a cracked pot!!

MOTIVES

What motivates you in life, what are you looking for,
What is your passion, what is your desire?
God created us out of love, it should be Him we seek,
We should give Him praise and glory, every time we speak.
God doesn't want us to be obligated, by our religion or our fear,
He wants us to serve Him out of love, He wants us to keep Him near.
If all He wanted was adoration, He could command the rocks to adore,
But He wants to share His love with all, to be one with Him forever more!
God gives us all a will to choose, we can serve Him or turn away,
He will not force His will upon us, we must choose to stay.
If we only serve Him out of obligation, or the fear of hell,
How can others see His peace and love, how can His glory we tell?
No, God doesn't want a bunch of robots, crying, "Holy is Your name",
He wants to share His joy and love, this is why Jesus came!
So examine your hearts, what is your passion, what motivates your drive,
And if it's not the love of God, then towards it you must strive.
For to know God is to love Him, and if you love Him you become one,
This should be your motivation, for everything you've done!!

Mike E. Robart

MATHEW 11, 28-30

Come to me all you who are weary and tired,
I will give you rest.
Take My yoke upon your shoulders and learn
from Me, for I am gentle and humble of heart.
For My yoke is easy and My burden light!

JOHN 3, 16-18

God so loved the world that He gave
His only begotten Son,
That who so ever believed in Him may not die,
but may have eternal life.
God did not send the Son to condemn the world,
but that the world might be saved through Him.
Whoever believes in Him shall have life everlasting,
but whoever does not believe is already condemned.

MARK 2, 17

People who are healthy do not need a doctor,
sick people do,
I have come to call the sinners, not the self-righteous.

DON'T DIE WITH YOUR MUSIC STILL IN YOU

God gives us all, a task we are to perform,
It may be to witness, or help a brother through a storm.
To some He gives voices, they are to praise His name,
To others He gives knowledge, they tell why Jesus came.
Some have the gift of prophecy, they tell what the future will hold,
Others He gives guidance, and our very lives they mold.
To some He gives healing, they fix our hurt and pain,
Jesus came to give Salvation, the reason He was slain !
What kind of music did God put inside of you,
What's your special talent, God wants to use you too !
Some go through life never experiencing, the gift God gives us all,
Some turn their heads and walk away, pretending not to hear His call.
Others say, "I'll get around to it, I've too much to do today".
What kind of music is in your heart, what song will you play?
A talent is something special, it's a gift that we must share,
It's a loving feeling in our heart, showing others that we care.
You may not change the world, but you can change someone's point of view,
Give your talents away, don't die with your music still in you !!

Mike E. Robart

I EXIST FOR YOU

On my own I am nothing, without you I would not exist,
You created me out of love, but yet I still insist.
I expect You to give me all, I keep a list for You to fill,
I talk to You like you're a servant, my wish You must instill.
My pride goes before me, look what I have done,
Then You lovingly remind me, it's about Jesus Christ, Your Son!
I was created for Your glory, I exist because of You,
I was saved by Jesus' sufferings, not the works I do.
Sometimes I think it's all about me, I forget why I was created,
Then You remind me of Your Son, and His life should be imitated.
God made man, He showed us the way, now we must do our part,
We must tell others of Your glory, express the love that is in our heart.
Without You I would not exist, I am because You are,
My soul longs for You oh God, this is what I was created for!
So I give You all the glory, may my love be pure and true,
And I lift Your name on high oh God, because I exist for YOU !!

WHY DO WE SIN

What drives us from You oh Lord, why do we sin,
What makes us turn away from You, can we start out new again?
I know how Adam and Eve felt, when they were tempted by Lucifer,
We try to lay all the blame on him, but the truth we must concur.
We each are given a will, it's up to us to choose,
We can't blame no one else, if heaven we do loose.
When I am drawn to sin, I could turn and walk away,
But sometimes I am weak, and the consequences I must pay.
I'm no longer walking in Your will, I miss Your presence so,
That's when I bow and ask for mercy, and You give it that I may grow.
And yet in the same situation I am drawn again,
I choose to stay instead of run away, and I fall back into sin.
It seems that I would learn, the outcome is the same,
I try to say it's the devil, he is all the blame.
 But down deep inside I know, it was I who chose to do wrong,
You were there by my side, but I failed to ask You to make me strong.
So I have no one to blame, the choices I make are my own,
But Father I'm so thankful, for all the mercy You have shown.
I don't see how You can forgive me, every time I fall,
I don't see how You can lift me up, every time I call.
So Father I come to You in adoration, I lift Your name on high,
I don't have the answer for sin, but still I question why?
But I know it's all a part, of the great plan we must fulfill,
And that is why I bow to You, and try once again to do Your will !!

Mike E. Robart

I JUST KEEP HAMMERING AWAY

I know when I've done wrong, it just don't feel right,
I have this feeling that I have hurt You, I'm no longer in Your light.
I know when I am tempted, I just need to call Your name,
But I turn my back and walk away, forgetting why You came !
It's as though I have that hammer, I'm nailing You to the cross,
I want to stop but I can't help it, I'm at such a loss.
I take pleasure in doing wrong, even though it caused You pain,
I forget about Your suffering, and the reason why You were slain.
I want to pull out those nails, that are in Your hands and feet,
I want to tell how You saved me, to everyone that I meet.
But yet when I am tempted, I reach for the hammer again,
Why can't I be strong, and just walk away from sin?
I tell myself I'm only human, but that is no excuse,
I placed those stripes upon Your back, I gave You such abuse !
It seems when I am tempted, it becomes only about me,
I forget about the pain and sorrow, You suffered upon that tree.
Now I fall down on my knees, I don't know what to say,
I want to ask for Your forgiveness, forgive me for hammering away.
Jesus You are so merciful, how can You love me like You do,
Then I remember what You said, it's not about me but You !
I came to save the lost and sinners, it's still true today,
I came that you may live, to take your sin away.
And though I just keep hammering, being good is really hard,
Thank You Jesus, You are my Savior, You are my Loving Lord !!

WHEN YOU CAN'T SEE GOD TRUST HIM ANYWAY

When life's trials get you down, you have no place to turn,
Trust in God to get you through, this I had to learn.
Life is like a window pane, you look out and all is clear,
Your view is unobstructed, everything seems so near.
But along comes trials and heartaches, putting cracks in your window pane,
It gets a little harder to see, but the view will still remain.
Then your life is turned upside down, you loose a child, a spouse, a friend,
Your life now seems so empty, you wish the pain would end.
Your window pane now becomes shattered, you can no longer see out,
You question God, "Why me Lord, is this what life's about"?
You can no longer see God, it's like the view that you once had,
This is when you must trust Him, He'll give you peace that makes you glad,
It's like the view through your shattered glass, you may not see it but it is there,
If you will only trust in God, your pain He wants to share.
He is there though we cannot see Him, His grace, His love, His power,
And if we will learn to trust in Him, He will give us what our heart desires.
To be one with God, to share in His love, what a joy that will be,
When we finally get to heaven, and our Father we will see !!

Mike E. Robart

REVELATIONS 22, 7, 13, 21

Remember, I am coming soon! Happy the man who heeds the prophetic message of this book!

I am the Alpha and the Omega, the First and the Last, the Beginning and the End! Happy are those who have washed their robes so as to have free access to the tree of life and enter through it's gates!

The grace of the Lord Jesus be with you all. AMEN

THE CROSS

When you look upon the cross, what exactly do you see,
I was raised a Catholic, and Christ's image was there for me.
I saw the crown of thorns, that pierced His head and brow,
I saw His wounded side, the suffering He endured somehow.
I saw the nails in His hands and feet, the stripes upon His back,
I saw the hurt that He went through, but love He did not lack!
He died upon that tree, He took our place our sin,
He suffered all to set us free, so we can live again.
And here when I look upon the cross, He's no longer there,
He arose to be with our Father, but I remember the pain He had to bear.
How can you look upon the cross, and not know His love for all,
How can you turn and walk away, pretending not to hear His call?
Jesus died that we may live, He arose to give us life,
He suffered all so we don't have too, He took away our strife.
The Cross is a symbol of Salvation, it's a choice that you must make,
Jesus died but He's coming back again, our spirits He will take.
Don't put it off and get left behind, Jesus cares for you,
Let the Cross be a symbol, of all that Christ's been through !!

Mike E. Robart

MY JOY IS NOT SOMEONE ELSES RESPONSIBILITY

Does your joy depend, upon someone else in your life,
Would you like to have more happiness, less strife?
You can blame it on your family, blame it on a friend,
But only you are responsible, in the very end!
You have a will to choose, you know wrong and right,
You can stay or turn and go, when you start to feel uptight.
You can argue, say unkind words, but what good will that do,
Or turn and walk away, it's really up to you!
You're always making choices, which way should I go,
It's up to you to decide, which will help you grow.
You know what makes you happy, you know what makes you sad,
So why not try to do the things, that make others glad.
When you're tired and feeling low, do you just mope around,
This is when the devil attacks, he loves to keep you down.
No you must choose to lift your spirit, hold your head up high,
Jesus lives inside me, He hears me when I cry!
I have a choice, I have a will, I'm responsible for my joy,
And Jesus is just a prayer away, His help He will employ.
So take responsibility, for the things you do,
Your joy does not depend on others, it depends on YOU !!

NOT MY WILL BUT YOURS BE DONE

How many times have we heard these words, they sound awful good,
But how many times do we do our wills, instead of what we should.
It seems our wills are more important, we turn and walk away,
Why can't we just follow You, and in Your love we'll always stay!
Problems seem to disappear, when I am in Your grace,
But when I turn and do my will, I have mountains I must face.
Why am I so human, I always want my way,
Why can't I be more like You, Jesus still lives today.
He taught us how we should live, putting others first,
But yet I want my will be done, which sometimes brings out the worst.
Father I know it's not about me, and I should be living for You,
Please don't get too upset with me, when I don't do what I should do.
I know You are a merciful Father, Your ways are higher than our own,
Let not my will be done, but Your will be known.
And give me the grace to do the things, that You place in my heart,
And give me the courage to lead the way, show me where to start.
And let me be more like You, and Jesus Christ Your Son,
For I know it's not about my will, but let Your will be done !!

Mike E. Robart

HE CAN WORK IT OUT

I give this problem to You oh God, that's so easy to say,
I trust in You to work it out, I will follow Your way.
The words are hardly out of our mouth, and you begin to worry,
I wonder if God heard me, I wonder how long He'll be.
Then along comes Satan planting ideas, and you begin to fret,
God are You too busy, why haven't You solved them yet?
Then you start thinking of things you can do, things you haven't tried,
God do You care how I'm hurting, all the pressures I have inside.
Your trust in Him who created the world, now begins to fade,
You're willing to try almost anything, but you are so afraid.
So you turn back to God and say again, I can't do this on my own,
I give my problem back to You, ease the pain that I've known.
I trust in You to work it out, I will follow Your way,
But when it's not solved in a week or so, you begin to say.
I haven't tried this, I think it will work, so you start out again,
But when that fails too you realize, I'm back where I've already been!
How many times do we try on our own, how many times must we fall,
How many heartaches must we endure, till we follow Gods call?
We say we trust in Him, when will we ever learn,
He can solve our problems, take away all our concern.
Next time you're faced with more than you can bear, turn to our God most high,
Truly give your problems to Him, you don't even have to try.
For He is capable to handle any situation, He really cares about you,
Things may seem impossible to us, but there is nothing God can't do!!

God's Light Shines Forth

A LOVE LETTER FROM JESUS

How are you My child, I have missed hearing from you,
I just wanted to let you know, I care about all you do.
You're always so busy with work or play, I haven't heard from you in a while,
I could come and rule your life, but this is not My style.
I wait for you to come to Me, I have so much to give,
I long for the day you open your heart, so there I may live!
I see you every morning, rushing out for another day,
How I wish you would talk to me, take a moment and pray.
I wake you with the rising sun, I give the moon to shine at night,
If only you would ask Me in, this would give Me such delight.
I have so much love I want to share, I try to bless you everyday,
My beauty is all around you, I try to light your way.
I whisper it to you in the leaves, I let you smell it in the flowers,
But I cannot force My love on you, even with My heavenly powers.
I know it's really hard on Earth, I've been there before,
I felt the pain, I know the hurt, it's something I can't ignore.
But I just wanted to let you know, you're always on my mind,
And I wait for you to open your heart, as I wait for all mankind.
Eternity is waiting, heaven is yours, to all who believe in us,
God the Father, the Holy Spirit, and your friend always, JESUS!!

PSALM 30: 2

I cry out to the Lord an He heals me!

PROVERBS 17: 23

A joyful heart is the health of the body, but a depressed Spirit dries up the bones.

1 PETER 2: 24

He Himself bore my sins in His body on the tree, so that I might die to sin and live for righteousness; by His wounds we are healed.

JEREMIAH 30: 17

The Lord has declared that He will restore me to health and heal my wounds.

THERAPY FOR THE HEART

We have therapy for all our sickness, for our aches and pain,
But what about the heart, should it remain the same?
God speaks to us through our hearts, some are made of stone,
He never can get through to us and make His wishes known.
While other hearts are warm and open, looking for the best,
Wanting to help those they meet, they are different than the rest.
How can you turn a hard heart, into one that shares,
First you must love yourself and show others that you care.
Then you need to read Gods word, let the stories melt away,
The calloused hearts will often soften, by what God has to say!
By being an example to those around you, they will want you possess,
Then you can share your heart with them, and bring them happiness.
God works in mysterious ways, is He calling out to you?
Therapy for the heart is something everyone can do!
So why not start today, open your heart receive Gods word,
Your life will get much better, if you practice what you've heard!!

Mike E. Robart

A PRAYER FOR HEALING

Father God in heaven, there is no one like You,
You have control, of all our lives, in all we say and do.
You are a Mighty and Merciful God, Your power is unsurpassed,
You always was, You always will be, forever will You last!
I come to You with a heavy burden, in the name of Jesus Your Son,
I ask for a healing miracle, just like Jesus done.
Jesus cured the lame, gave sight to the blind, even resurrected the dead,
By His stripes, we are healed, this is what the bible said.
Where two or more are gathered, and praying in My Name,
There I will be too, this is why Jesus came.
Satan brings sickness to our bodies, he tries to steal our soul,
He wants to keep us, sad and depressed, this is really his goal.
But Jesus died that we may live, He defeated Satan and all his power,
We have to believe and trust in Jesus, tell God what our hearts desire.
Father You created this world from nothing, our hope is in Your hands,
You still work miracles, for Your Glory, we are part of all Your plans.
So Father I ask, with a humble heart, show me now Your will,
I accept whatever You decide, and I will love You still!
For without You Father beside me, my hope would disappear,
Without Your love to guide me, I would live in fear.
Jesus is my Lord and Savior, there is nothing He can't do,
He is living, in my heart, so we are a part of You.
So Father God in heaven, hear our humble cry,
Deliver us from this burden, and may we never question why!

MIRACLES STILL HAPPEN

Miracles happen every day, most we never see,
They happen all around us, we had one in our family!
My niece was given, little hope, she lay lifeless in her bed,
She has just days, or hours to live, this is what the doctors said.
But our lives are not our own, they are in Gods hand,
And He will not, take us home, till we do all that He has planned.
We prayed for a Miracle to happen, then before our very eyes,
God brought her back to us, much to our surprise.
We never know what the future holds, so we must learn to trust,
Put our hopes, in God above, faith in Him is a must.
To those who do not know Him, life is like a game,
We all start out as sinners, this is why Jesus came.
When we accept Him in our lives, they'll seem to turn around,
God can work our problems out, this is what I've found.
But we must learn to trust, His ways are higher than our own,
And if we follow, His direction, we'll reap what He has sown.
So yes, Miracles still happen, keep an open mind,
They may not be, as grand as ours, some are hard to find.
But Jesus works today, like He has in days gone by,
Put your hope and trust in Him, and on Him always rely!!

Mike E. Robart

BE HAPPY WITH YOURSELF

Remember always, we must live with some of the people part of our life,
We must live with a few of the people most of our life,
But we must live with ourselves all our life!
We must learn to respect and love ourselves, or how can we show others what we don't possess,
How can we help our fellow brothers, if our own life is a mess?
Some people are quick to judge and criticize, while others show true concern,
The faith and love we have in our heart. Is something we must learn.
Faith comes from God, it's a matter of trust, in something that cannot be seen,
Love is a feeling that builds in our heart, it can grow or turn to hate unseen.
If we don't first love ourselves, how can we give love away,
The feeling we hold deep in our heart, is seen by what we do and say.
God gives us all a will to choose, what choices will you make,
How do you feel about yourself, is there a different road you need to take?
Sit down and take time, go over your life, is there something you don't understand
Ask God for help, because if you're not happy, you'll never receive all that God has planned!!

A PRAYER OF BEAUTY

I look up in the heavens, and Your beauty shines forth on me,
You paint the sunsets, on the clouds, for all the world to see.
You place the stars, in the heavenly bodies, they twinkle in the night,
The sun in all its awesome glory, fills our world with light.
The clouds take shapes and forms, some are white, others gray,
If you're lucky, you will see the rainbow, God's promise to this day.
The morning sunrise, brings many colors, a beauty to behold,
But this is nothing, compared to heaven, this is what I'm told!
Your beauty is all around us Father, it's every where I look,
The deep blue ocean waters, or the babbling of a brook.
How can we look, at the flowers and trees, and the beauty of the hills,
How can we, not feel Your Love, how can we not do Your will?
I guess too many times, we are burdened, we all have trials to face,
We let our problems, get us down, we are caught in life's rat race.
We forget about, Your love for us, we can no longer see Your beauty,
Instead of enjoying our life on earth, it now becomes our duty.
Father, let this be my prayer, may Your beauty I always see,
And may I give, all glory to You, for all I'll ever be.
For without You Father, in my life, it would be empty, cold and black,
But with You Father, I am happy and can't wait till Jesus comes back!!

PROVERBS 18:21

The power of life or death are in the tongue, and they who indulge in it shall eat the fruit of it.

PROVERBS 3: 13-15

Happy is the man who finds wisdom, and the man who gains understanding; for her proceeds are better than the profits of silver, and her gain than fine gold. She is more precious than rubies, and all the things you may desire cannot compare to her.

In the bible Jesus used parables to tell a story, in the next five poems I use short stories and put them into poetry to express a point. Sometimes we use words to hurt people, words can destroy someone's character so we have to watch what we say. Many times they are just spoken, not to do harm, but other people take them the wrong way, it is very easy to be misunderstood.

THE NEW CORVETTE

There was a rich man who had a son, he met his every need,
The son was about to graduate, so he began to plead.
Father buy me a new corvette, to show how much you love me,
The father just smiled and hugged him tight, saying "We'll see!"
Upon graduation the son couldn't wait, he knew what was in store,
But dad just gave him one small package, nothing more!
As the son began to open the box, all he saw was a book,
It said "Holy Bible", you should have seen that sons look!
He threw it down at his fathers feet, I never want to see you again,
He left that day, he never called, lived a life of sin.
Many years later he got a call from his mother, your dad has passed away,
Won't you please come back home, I have so much to say.
The son returned for his mothers sake, they began to talk,
She told him how his father loved him, how it hurt to see him walk.
How his father was a proud man, he wanted to call but never did,
Now it was too late, I would have told you, but he forbid!
The son began to feel remorse, as he headed for his old room,
He remembered all the happy times, before his days were doomed.
He saw the box upon the shelf, he took the bible out,
He read the note taped inside, "This is what life's about."
He felt a lump and turned the page, then he saw the key,
'The corvette is in the shed out back, always remember me!'
How many years have you wasted, our Father has so much to give,
But we must surrender, to His ways, if we are to live!!

Mike E. Robart

FEATHERS IN THE WIND

A catholic priest was visiting this young widow, several times a week,
As this went on for several months, the people began to speak.
Two elderly ladies with nothing to do, began to spread rumors around,
It wasn't long till the rumor was passed, to everyone in town!
Then it happened, the widow died, her story could be told,
She had cancer, but no one knew the priest was there to console.
The two old ladies came to him, and apologized for their actions,
They were sorry for making him, the center of attraction.
He gave them a pillow, full of feathers, take this up the hill,
And let them go, one by one, my wish you must fulfill.
They did as they were told, they returned with the empty pillowcase,
Now will you forgive us, you could see the sorrow in their face.
You must do one more thing, if you want me to forgive,
Go and gather each feather, and bring them to where I live.
But they said that's impossible, the winds have scattered them everywhere,
So it is with the rumors you told, didn't you even care?
What rumors are you spreading, whose life will they effect,
Words sometimes get twisted, their meanings are hard to detect.
So think before you speak, will this hurt someone in the end,
Your words too once spoken, become like Feathers In The Wind!!

THE HUNDRED DOLLAR BILL PRINCIPLE

If I had a crisp new one hundred dollar bill, would you want it?
What if I crumpled it all up, would you still want it?
What if I took it outside and stomped it in the mud?
Maybe I would rip it in a couple of places, what about then?
Most people would still take it, because it's value has not changed,
Even though it's dirty, crumpled, torn, it's appearance is re-arranged.
But it's value is still one hundred dollars!
Our value in Gods eyes is still the same, He created us like Him,
He loves us unconditionally, even when we become a problem.
We sin and are covered in stain,
But Jesus makes us whole again!
We make up stories, lie, cheat, and deceive,
But God forgets it all, if only Jesus we receive.
Our lives get torn by heartaches, people let us down,
Our situations sometimes seem hopeless, it's as if we are about to drown.
But in Gods eyes, our value has not changed a bit,
So He reaches down to help us out, keeps our candle lit!
He keeps the desire, in our heart, to be one with Him once more,
Cause our value is still the same, we are His forever more!!

Mike E. Robart

THREE SHATTERED DREAMS

In Jerusalem long ago stood three trees, each had a dream,
The olive tree wanted to become a treasure chest, with gold around it's seem.
The oak tree dreamed of becoming a ship, to carry kings to war,
The pine tree dreamed of standing tall, but none got very far!
The olive tree was made into a trough, in which animals were fed,
The oak tree became only a small fishing boat, it's dream now was dead.
The pine tree in all it's mighty grandeur, reaching to the sky,
Was struck by lightening, then cut down, no one can say why.
Three dreams shattered, not one came true, but God had other plans,
He would bring them greater glory, I hope you'll understand.
The olive tree now the trough, held baby Jesus when He was born,
The oak tree now the fishing boat, carried Jesus in the storm.
The pine tree once tall and mighty, was made into a cross,
He held the precious body of Jesus, now it's a symbol of our loss.
Dreams get shattered, we don't always understand, but we must learn to trust,
God has our lives planned out for us, obedience is a must!
If we will only let Him lead us, He has better days ahead,
He places things upon our heart, His word we need to spread!!

GOOD LUCK OR BAD

There was an old Chinaman who had a horse, people tried to buy it everyday,
Then one night it got out, and the stallion ran away.
His neighbors came over saying, "What bad luck, you could have sold him for such a gain."
The Chinaman said, "How do you know it's bad, is this the reason you came?"
The next day his stallion returned along with thirteen wild horses to eat,
The son snuck out and closed the gate, thinking wow, this is neat!
His neighbors heard and came back again, "What good luck you've had,"
The Chinaman said, "How do you know it's good, it could also be bad."
Later that week his son was breaking the horses got thrown off and broke his back
The neighbors heard of his misfortune and came over cause the future looked black.
"Your luck is definitely bad," they said, but the Chinaman would not agree,
"How do you know if it's bad or good, the future you cannot see!
Only God knows what the future holds, we must learn to trust,
We must learn to follow His ways, surrender to Him is a must."
Several months went by and there came a war, all able bodied young men must go,
But the son of the Chinaman could not answer the call, the others now envied him so!
His neighbors came over, "Your luck is now good, our sons will never return,"
The Chinaman just scratched his head, "When will they ever learn?"
God has our futures planned out, if we will only obey,
But we must learn to trust in Him, each and every day!!

PSALM 31: 7

I am overcome with joy because of God's unfailing love, for He sees my troubles, and He cares about the anguish of my soul.

PSALM 23: 1-4

The Lord is my shepherd; I shall not want, in green pastures He gives me rest. Besides restful waters He leads me, He guides me in right paths for His names sake. Even though I walk in the valley, I will fear no evil for He is at my side to protect and guide me. With His rod and staff He gives me courage.

These next five poems are meant to give relief in a difficult time, a time we will all experience at some point in our life. Death is something we cannot escape, but it is so much easier for those who believe in Jesus and His resurrection. Death to a Christian is merely a passing from this human life to a spiritual life. We are all created by God and this life on Earth is only a test, we must prove our love for God. For God so loved the world that He gave His only begotten Son, that whosoever believed in Him shall not perish but have eternal life. This is our goal! My goal is to take as many people with me as I can, with the help of God above.

IN TIMES LIKE THESE

In times like these we come together, to comfort and console,
The pain seems so unbearable, it reaches our very soul.
We sometimes question, "Why me Lord, have we been so bad?"
But God's been through it all Himself, He knows the hurts we had.
You see, God is there beside you, He has felt the hurt, the pain,
And though He is God He could do nothing, when His Son was slain.
You may think God don't care for us, or why would He allow,
This suffering to come upon us, where is He right now?
I want to re-assure you, God knows your feelings of despair,
And He would like to talk to you, come to Him in prayer.
He can lift your heavy burden, He can calm your troubled heart,
But He won't do it on His own, it's up to you to start!
So in this time of sorrow, take a moment to pray,
You don't have to go through this alone, let God lead the way.
He'll give you His comfort and peace, He is there for you,
Lean on and trust in Him, He will get you through.
In times like these we feel alone, like no one really cares,
But God is there, God is LOVE, this love He wants to share!
Just cast your cares upon Him, feel the warmth of His embrace,
You are not alone, receive His loving grace.
As you feel His presence all around, fall down on your knees,
He'll lift you up, because He really cares, in such a time as these!!

Mike E. Robart

SAFELY HOME

You see what was once my home, lying there before you,
I no longer need that body, to do the things I do.
I am up in heaven, if you could only see me now,
I am safely home, my journey is complete somehow.
I wish you all could join me, but God has other plans,
I once felt the hurt you're going through, it seems more than you can stand.
Just cast your cares upon our Father, He is there in time of need,
He will give you comfort and hope, a peace of mind indeed.
Our Father knows what we go through, He's been there before,
He had to watch His Son die, to even up the score.
Now Jesus lives and so do I, you all can live again,
Ask Jesus to come and live inside, be sorry for your sins.
If you could only see this place, only feel this peace,
Love is everywhere you turn, it will never cease.
When I was alive, I could never comprehend, what heaven had in store,
But now that I am living here, it is so much more.
I am truly happy, and no longer will I roam,
For I have reached my destination, I am Safely Home!!

GONE BUT NOT FORGOTTEN

You are gone but not forgotten, in our hearts you will remain,
You are a loss to us on Earth, but God has much to gain.
Your memories are everywhere I turn, I look but you're not there,
I find myself talking to you, telling you how much I care.
I still feel you in my heart, how it hurt to see you go,
But God has re-assured me, you're in a better place I know.
But still the pain goes on, He says this too will heal,
Death is something we all experience, this is part of the deal.
We were created to be with God, life is part of His plan,
He had to feel what we feel, that's why He became Man!
Now He knows what we go through, that's why He's always there,
He will never give us, more than we can bare.
When will this pain go away, I reach out but you are gone,
I try remembering the happy times, this is how I get things done.
I feel your presence in my life, but now on God I must depend,
We'll be together soon I know, but till then you will be gone, but not forgotten!!

Mike E. Robart

WITHOUT EXPANATION

Things happen in this life, we have no explanation,
We cannot comprehend, or know every situation.
This is when we must trust our God, He will get us through,
We must lean on those around us, for the burden is too great for you.
But still we question, "Why God, how can this be,
How can I accept this fact and face reality"?
We don't have all the answers, right now you are filled with grief,
But God with all His infinite love, will give us sweet relief.
He knows the emptiness that you feel, the hurt, the sorrow, the pain,
He felt what we go through, when Jesus His Son was slain.
But we are only human, we cannot understand,
Now more than ever we must trust in Him, and all that He has planned.
But still we question why, why did it have to be this way,
Only God has all the answers, but we will see one day.
For there is more than this life on Earth, heaven awaits us all,
Your loved one is gone, but you'll see her again, she answered Jesus' call!
Only time will heal the hurt, but her memories are always there,
Recall the good times that you had, these you'll want to share.
And know in your heart she lives again, and you will see her once more,
And you will be re-united, in heaven forevermore.!!

IF ONLY YOU COULD SEE HEAVEN

If only you could see heaven, how happy you would be,
You would no longer grieve, knowing I was here for eternity.
Once I felt the pain, that you're going through,
But heaven is a better place, how I wish I could share it with you.
I can see the hurt and sorrow, I realize the burden you must bare,
But if you trust in Jesus, this pain He will share.
In this difficult time, your burden seems to heavy to carry,
But our Father up in heaven, gives peace to those who are weary.
How I wish you could see heaven, your spirit it would lift,
If I could grant you just one wish, this would be my gift!
For up in heaven peace abounds, love is all you feel,
Happiness on Earth comes and goes, but in heaven it is real.
Heaven is indescribable, it's beauty is unsurpassed,
You have to be here to feel the love, forever will it last.
So please don't grieve for me, may God replace your sorrow with peace,
And may you know the love I feel, for it will never cease.
And I can't wait till you get here with me, what joy there will be,
Together forever, in Gods court, for all eternity!!

Mike E. Robart

ISAIAH 40: 31

As I wait for the Lord I shall change and renew my strength and power; I shall lift my wings and mount up as eagles; I shall run and not be weary, I shall walk and not faint or become tired.

DEUTERONOMY 10: 12

What does the Lord my God require of me but to fear the Lord my God, that is to walk in all His ways, and to love Him, and to serve Him with all my heart and mind, my entire being.

In these next five poems I try to express the relationship we should have with God, He loves us and cares for us and wants only the best for us. We must learn to trust and rely on Him at all times and He will never let us down. God has our life planned out if we would only let Him have control, but to often we think we can do a better job sometimes we have to learn the hard way!

IN HIS PRESENCE

I used to think when I did wrong, God was out to get me,
But now He has opened my eyes, that I may clearly see.
He loves us just the same, whether we do right or wrong,
Now I truly see, it's His love that makes us strong.
But yet it amazes me how He loves me in such a way,
That when I come to Him saying "I'm Sorry", in His grace I'll stay!
Now I know that sin offends Him, and I can't live with that,
I never want to hurt my God, so He meets me where I'm at.
When I'm in a sinful state, He reaches down and pulls me near,
He assures me He still loves me, that I have nothing to fear.
How can God love me when I do wrong, I cannot understand,
How could He take the sins of all, and become the Son Of Man?
Maybe that day when I stand in His presence, I'll finally comprehend,
Just how great His love is for us, and it will never end!
We serve a Mighty and Awesome God, His love has no bound,
He wants to share His love with us, and spread it all around.
So now when I am tempted I stop and think, what would Jesus do,
I think about His pain and suffering, and all that He's been through.
I try to turn and walk away, but there are times when I still fall,
That is when God embraces me, and I beckon to His call.
This is when I feel His love the most, there I want to remain,
In the presence of a loving God, never do I want to hurt Him again!!

Mike E. Robart

YOU ARE NO SURPRISE TO GOD

You say you can't come to God now, my life is full of sin,
You are no surprise to God, He knows every where you've been.
He knows what your future holds, He has it all planned out,
But you must submit, to His will, trust Him, without doubt.
God loves us all the same, we all are born in sin,
But He will give us His grace, to start out new again.
He sent His Son to Earth, to die in our place,
And we must accept Jesus, as our Savior, if we are to look upon His Face!
It doesn't matter, how we have lived, our past will be forgotten,
What will your future hold, if you accept Jesus, God's own Son?
Don't be afraid to Ask Him in, let Him have control,
Jesus is waiting, in heaven for you, let that be your goal.
Don't pretend, you can't hear Him calling, His arms are open wide,
He's calling out your name, won't you let Him come inside?
Don't feel you have to run from Jesus, open up your eyes,
Remember God knows all, to Him, you are no surprise!!

YOU DO YOUR BEST- I'LL DO THE REST

Father, You are Mighty, Merciful, Forgiving, All Loving,
I am weak, a sinner, but I am sorrowful as I come to You with nothing.
I try to do what is right, but so many times I fall short,
Then I am filled with sorrow, and I ask for a brand new start.
I have a choice in all I do, so many times I choose wrong,
I try to impress people by my actions, I want to make them think I'm strong.
But on my own, I am helpless, that's when I turn to You,
And You show me mercy, once again, for all the things I do.
It seems that I would learn, from all the mistakes I make,
I thank You for being so forgiving, and that You never forsake.
Father I'll never comprehend, the depths of Your Love,
Till I meet You, face to face, in heaven, up above.
I try to bring You down to my level, but You are so much higher,
You try to lift me up, fill my heart with Love and desire.
Someday we'll meet I know, maybe then I'll understand,
Be able to grasp, Your Infinite Love, and all that You have planned.
But until then, I'll try to do what's right, I'll try to do my best,
And I will trust and follow You, and let You do the rest!!

Mike E. Robart

YOUR WILL

Father You led me into the wilderness, when I had lost my way,
You showed me the peace and joy of heaven, now I'm here to stay.
I don't know where my journey will lead, my life has ups and downs,
But I know for sure when my life is through, You'll reward me with a crown.
I once was lost but now I've found, Your love I can't replace,
It keeps me going every day, till I look upon Your Face.
I trusted You when all hope was gone, and I had no place to turn,
You never let me walk alone, this I had to learn.
You led me down life's narrow paths, sometimes I didn't follow,
But You never did give up on me, nor fill my life with sorrow.
You gave me strength to carry on, even when I turned my back,
You always had someone special, to get me back on track.
So now I give my life to you, mold me like I was clay,
Put in my heart and mind and soul, the words You want me to say.
For Jesus Your Son has died for me, He took my place my sin,
He opened the gates of heaven, and invites all to come in!
He paid the price, once for all, He became the perfect Lamb,
Not everyone will accept His gift, but you can be sure I am.
So thank You Father for the gifts You gave, my life has been a thrill,
I give You praise, I give You glory, as I carry out Your will!!

SEEKING

Father You said, "Seek and you shall find, ask and you shall receive",
"Knock and the door shall be opened", this is what I believe.
I sought things but never found them, I asked but still I wait,
I knocked but the door remained closed, why am I in such a state?
Could it be what I am seeking, I already have, or don't really need,
Maybe what I'm asking, I only ask in greed.
The door that I want opened, could it be the door to my own heart,
That's the door I should have opened, from the very start!
Only I can open it, and ask You to come in,
But only You can save me, and cleanse me of my sin.
So Father I am seeking, and I'm asking for Your grace,
And I want You to live inside me, till I look upon Your face!!

Mike E. Robart

PSALM 95: 7,8

Today I will hear His voice and harden not my heart.

PSALM 27: 1

The Lord is my Light and my Salvation; whom shall I fear or dread? The Lord is the Refuge and Stronghold of my life, of whom shall I be afraid?

ISAIAH 41: 10

No weapon formed against me shall prosper, and every tongue that rises against me in judgment I shall show to be in the wrong. This is my inheritance because I am a servant of the Lord!

These last five poems covers from the beginning to the end and life in between. I hope in some way that these poems will touch your heart and if you don't already know Jesus it will help you decide to want to learn more. Life is a choice, we all must choose, open the door of your heart and allow Jesus to enter!

IN THE BEGINNING

In the beginning was God, He always was and always will be,
He created the Heavens and Earth, as well as you and me.
He took nothing and made what we have today,
So don't you think He may have a part, in what we do and say?
He created all the Angels, the good ones and the bad,
And when some turned against Him, it made Him very sad!
So God came up with a new idea, He created Man,
And gave each one a will to choose, that would be His plan.
He knew that most would turn away, but yet He was not through,
So He became a Man Himself, just like me and you.
He was born a baby, and grew just like us all,
He lived and laughed like each of us, till He got His call.
The devil knew that He was God, but he tempted Him the same,
Till that day upon the cross, his power He overcame!
Now Jesus reigns with His heavenly Father, over each and every one,
And we can reign in heaven too, by accepting Gods own Son!
So no matter where you are in life, it is not too late,
To accept Jesus as your Lord, but do not hesitate,
For He is coming back again, to take His children home,
And we will live in harmony, no longer will we roam.
The mansions and the streets of gold, will now be ours at last,
And we will walk with our heavenly Father, just like they did in the past!!

Mike E. Robart

RIGHT OR WRONG

Does sin drive us farther away, from Your loving open arms,
Or does it draw us nearer, as when we face life's storms.
I hang my head when I've done wrong, how can You love someone like me,
Then I think of what Jesus said, as He hung upon that tree.
"Father forgive them, for they know not what thou hast done,"
Then I realize, Jesus was Gods only begotten Son!
He died once for all our sins, He will not die again,
He paid the price for everyone, so we do not live in sin.
He cleansed our souls of all dark spots, washed them white as snow,
He'll come again to take us home, this I surely know!
He is my Lord and Savior, and I trust Him more each day,
And though I don't always do what's right, I know in His love, Ill always stay!!

HOLY-HOLY-HOLY

Holy, Holy, Holy, Holy is Your name,
Three persons in one Godhead, and yet You're all the same.
The Father, Son, and Holy Spirit, each has a special place,
But when we look upon You, we'll see one loving face.
The Father was the Creator, the Son died for our sins,
The Holy Spirit lives inside us, on Him you can depend.
Though separate yet together, three persons in one Godhead,
It's hard for me to understand, but this is what You said.
I AM, I WAS, I'LL ALWAYS BE, no beginning or no end,
You're here, You're there, You're everywhere, You come and go just like the wind!
But I feel You all around me, You're ever where I go,
Whether Father, Son, or Spirit, You keep my heart aglow.
So God I praise Your Holy Name, give honor to You too,
Holy, Holy, Holy, I'm nothing, without You!!

Mike E. Robart

GOD BELIEVES IN YOU-
HE CANT BE WRONG

God believes in you, He can't be wrong, He who made us all,
Isn't it God who lights our way, and picks us up each time we fall?
He leads each step that we take, He is in control,
He wants to share all things with us, that's why He gave us our soul.
If we will only trust Him, how can we go wrong,
The devil fills our hearts with fears, but God will make us strong.
God and you make a majority, who can be against us,
The devil once defeated, will turn and leave in disgust.
So how can One who gave us His Son, how can He not care,
Don't you think He believes in you, and His world He wants to share?
God makes no junk, He has a plan, and we must surely follow,
He will fill our hearts with love, and give us seeds to sow,
So next time you feel out of place, feel like you don't belong,
Remember God believes in you, and He is never wrong!!

THE END

When the end finally comes, and you draw your last breath,
Who's going to cry, at the news of your death?
Did you spend all your time, at work or at play,
Or did you take time, to stop and pray?
Was God number one, or two, or three,
Did He live in your heart, for others to see.
It's easy to get sidetracked, there's so much to do,
Is that what the people, are going to say about you?
Oh how he partied, the fun never stopped,
He laughed and he drank, till the day he dropped.
Or maybe you worked, long hours on the job,
Never seeing the tears, or hearing the sob.
Your family was there, but you never took the time,
You were important, you had a ladder to climb.
I'll go see Jason play ball, or watch Susie dance,
But what if something happens, and you never get the chance?
You live only once, the time flies by,
You don't know the day, or time you will die.
Stop, look, and listen, to your heart today,
It has something important, it's trying to say!
Only you can open it, and let Jesus inside,
Maybe it's time, you swallowed your pride.
Confess all your sins, we all have a few,
Is that what the Spirit, is asking you do?
Don't wait another day, it may never come,
Don't put it off, till tomorrow like some.
You may say, "I'm still young, I have places to go and see,
I'll get around to it, you can count on me!
I'm a pretty good guy, I do what is right,
Don't ask me, to accept Jesus tonight.
I'll live my life, and when the time gets near,

Mike E. Robart

I'll get right with God, I have nothing to fear".
But what if tonight, when you lay down to sleep,
Your life is required, and no one hears a peep.
You draw your last breath, your time has run out,
Will those who come to mourn you, have any doubt?
So live each day, like there's no tomorrow,
So those who love you, don't go through this sorrow.
With Jesus in your heart, when you go to rest,
Everyone will know, you gave it your best!!

Now that you have read these poems is there an area in your heart where God is speaking to you, have they touched you in any way? God uses different methods to reach His children, sometimes He has to use several. If I could help just one person choose Jesus, then the effort of these poems have paid off, my time will not have been wasted. People put off making important decisions, I'll get around to it tomorrow, but what if tomorrow doesn't come, for some it will be too late, don't be left behind. If you had a sickness that was threatening your body wouldn't you go and see if it could be treated or healed, people don't look at becoming saved in the same light, but actually it is more important than being healed, you have just so many days to spend on Earth, but you have an eternity to spend in heaven! Think about it, where are you going to go when you draw your last breath, it's a decision that only you can make, no one else is responsible for your salvation. The choice is YOUR'S , what is your choice??????

You may have been a church member for years, or you may have not ever stepped a foot into a church, but if you don't know where you will spend eternity say this simple prayer and mean it with all your heart.

Father, I am a sinner, I am sorry for all the wrongs I have ever done, I believe Jesus is Your Son and that He came to Earth and died for our sins, I accept Him now as my Lord and Savior, Come into my life and cleanse me. I believe You arose from the dead and that You will return to take your children home!

Some people may think, how can a simple prayer like this get me into heaven, you don't know all the things that I've done. It's not about what we've done, it's all about God and His Grace, no one is to bad that God will not forgive them if they come to Him with a contrite heart seeking His forgiveness. We are all the same in God's eyes, we are all sinners and it is only through His Grace we are made whole again, Jesus say's "I am the Way, the Truth and the Life, he who believes in Me shall never die, I came that man might be set free." So you see, it's not about what we have done, it's all about Him! Likewise there is nothing we can do to earn our own way into Heaven, we can go to church every day, be nice to everyone we meet, always do what is right but that will still not earn us Heaven. Jesus is the only way, by accepting Him as our Lord and Savior we become children of God and heirs to Heaven, but we still have to choose, no one else can make that decision for us. It all comes down to our choice, we choose where we want to spend Eternity. Whether or not you believe in God, or think it's all some fairy tale when you draw your last breath you will stand before Him. For many it will be to late, the decision they made on Earth will determine where they spend Eternity.

You may think if God is so good how could He send me to Hell? Remember, it was your choice, you decided, you had the chance to accept Jesus or turn and walk away. Everything we do in life is a choice, we can choose to do what's right, or we can choose what's wrong, that is why we are given a will and God cannot choose for us. So if your choice was to turn your back, you have no-one to blame but yourself.

My choice is Jesus, I am on my way to Heaven and I would like to take as many with me as possible. In these poems I tried to convey to you how much God loves you and cares for you. The Holy Spirit inspired me to write them, I am just an instrument, I give Him all the praise and glory. There were times when I didn't know what to say but then this thought would come into my head. I knew it had to be Him because I am just a sinner, and everyday person like all of you, I still do things wrong but I know that Jesus has already died for all my sins and I accept His Grace and Mercy and Forgiveness. That's what being Saved is all about, it's not about us, it's all about Him.

My one wish is that anyone who reads this book will come to know the peace and joy that I have received from writing it. May Gods Peace be with you all, may the choices you make be the right ones, may God bless you in all that you do.

Your Brother In Christ,

Mike

About the Author

I am a 56 year old utility worker who has been at his job for 32 years, I enjoy my work, it's always helping people who have some kind of problem. I served in the U.S. Navy for 4 years, served 2 terms in Vietnam, I really enjoyed seeing other people in other parts of the world, it was a very good learning experience. I am a Christian and I love talking about God and His love and goodness. I got started writing Christian poetry two years ago when I was watching the Hour Of Power with Dr. Schuller, the Holy Spirit put it on my heart to write some poems about his quotes and I just kept writing about things in my life. Now He is leading me to get them published, these poems are all about God and His love for all His children, we are all Gods children some of us just hasn't accepted it yet! It doesn't matter where you are in life, what you've done wrong, God is willing to accept you where you are if you are willing to accept His Son, Jesus Christ. Jesus has paid the price for all our sins and it is by Gods grace we are made new again, to those who don't know about this God maybe these poems will shed some light. I know it has brought me closer to Him by just writing them, I give Him all the praise and all the glory!!

Printed in the United States
127944LV00003B/62/A